CANUTE
AND THE
VIKINGS

Robin May

Illustrations by Gerry Wood

LIFE AND TIMES

Julius Caesar and the Romans
Alfred the Great and the Saxons
Canute and the Vikings
William the Conqueror and the Normans
Richard the Lionheart and the Crusades
Columbus and the Age of Exploration
Elizabeth I and Tudor England
Oliver Cromwell and the Civil War

Further titles are in preparation

First published in 1984 by
Wayland (Publishers) Ltd,
49 Lansdowne Place, Hove,
East Sussex BN3 1HF, England

© Copyright 1984 Wayland (Publishers) Ltd

ISBN 0 85078 471 9

Phototypeset by Planagraphic Typesetters Ltd
Printed in Italy by G. Canale & C.S.p.A., Turin
Bound in the U.K. by The Pitman Press, Bath

Contents

1 THE STORY OF CANUTE

A stormy childhood

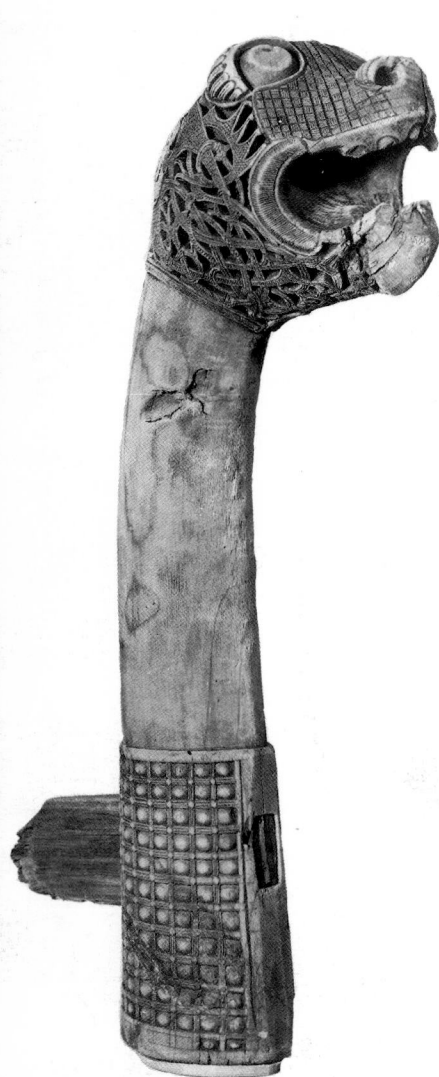

The story is often told of how King Canute's feet were soaked when the waves ignored his command to retreat. His courtiers had wanted to flatter him, saying that even the waves would obey him. He showed them that he could not command the waves — that although he was a king, he was not all-powerful.

This story is based on a document written much later, and may be sheer invention. Yet one thing is certain. Canute, once a bloodthirsty Viking warrior, became one of the best of English monarchs.

Born about AD 994, Canute (or Cnut) was the youngest son of King Swein Forkbeard of Denmark, a ferocious Viking leader. For many years before Canute's birth, Saxon England had been ravaged by Viking raiders. Saxon kings had struggled to repel them, but like the sea, their tide could not be turned back. Over the years, many Vikings (often called Danes because the Vikings that harassed England were mostly from Denmark) had settled to live alongside the Saxons who had once been their enemies. But the peace had not lasted long.

When Canute was young, England was ruled by the weak Ethelred the Unready. This weakness was an invitation to the Vikings, who resumed their raids in 980. Canute's father, Swein, spearheaded these attacks in the hope of easy plunder. Ethelred tried to bribe the invaders to stay away, but the attacks continued.

In desperation, Ethelred ordered all Vikings in England to be slaughtered in the notorious Massacre of St Brice's Day in 1002. One of the dead was Swein's sister, Gunnhild. In a rage, Swein swore a bloody revenge and

Above *The prow of a Viking longship, carved like a dragon to strike terror into the hearts of their enemies.*

Above *Canute's followers believed that the king had the power to stop the tide from rising. He proved them wrong — and got soaked in the process.*

Right *The king from a set of Viking walrus ivory chessmen, found on the Isle of Lewis in the Outer Hebrides in the twelfth century.*

he launched a series of furious attacks. By the time of his death in 1014, Swein was master of most of England, although Ethelred was still officially king. Canute's harsh upbringing made him familiar with violence and the importance of firm government.

Above *This stone slab from a tomb, showing a lion and a snake, was found in St. Paul's Churchyard and dates back to Canute's time.*

A silver coin minted during Canute's reign.

The fight for England's crown

When Canute visited England for the first time in 1013, the land he was to govern so well lay in ruins. A strong king was needed. The choice lay with the people of England, both Vikings and Saxons. They had divided loyalties. Some continued to support Ethelred as the rightful king, but others preferred Canute because he was the stronger of the two men.

Canute was declared king by his troops at Gainsborough in Lincolnshire, where he was holding a number of hostages prisoner. Ethelred, in a rare moment of action, marched his army north, and forced Canute to put to sea. In an act of great barbarity, Canute put the hostages ashore on the Kentish coast having first ordered that their noses and hands be cut off. He then sailed to Denmark to build up another army for the reconquest of England.

Above *On the death of Edmund Ironside, Canute became the undisputed King of England, and was crowned early in 1017.*

By the autumn of 1015, Canute was back on English soil. A few months later, Ethelred died. Canute was left to face a more formidable foe — Ethelred's son, the valiant Edmund Ironside, leader of the resistance to the Danes.

Londoners chose Edmund as their king, but Earl Eadric of Mercia joined Canute. Despite a courageous struggle, Edmund's supporters were heavily defeated at the Battle of Ashingdon in 1016. The two young men agreed to divide the kingdom: Canute to take Mercia, and Edmund to govern Wessex.

But then Edmund died suddenly, possibly murdered. By the end of 1016 Canute was recognized as the king of all England. To the amazement of Englishmen, he was a much wiser king than his bloodthirsty life had suggested he would be.

Mighty monarch

Above *Canute and his Queen Emma present a cross to Hyde Abbey, Winchester, from a book written at the time.*

Canute looked every inch a king. A contemporary account describes him as a 'very tall and strong and handsome man . . . he was generous, a great warrior, very valiant, very victorious and a man of great luck in everything connected with power.' In his dealings with England, he showed tact and strength.

To bring peace to his divided kingdom, Canute agreed to keep the laws of Edgar, the last great English king, who had died in 975. He also grasped the importance of having the Church on his side and allied himself with Wulfstan, the powerful Archbishop of York.

The once ferocious raider soon became a devoted Christian. Canute helped monasteries, respected the memory of English saints, even those slain by Vikings, and gave his support to poets and minstrels. A highlight of his reign was his pilgrimage to Rome in 1026 to visit Pope John XIX.

Despite Canute's conversion to Christianity, his prowess as a warrior remained great. He became King of Denmark in 1018, and of Norway too when his enemy, Olaf II, was killed in the Battle of Stiklestad in 1030. As King of England, Norway and Denmark, Canute was the most powerful monarch in northern Europe.

Canute's favoured home was England. He died there, at Shaftesbury in Dorset, in 1035. His reign was a time of peace and prosperity for England. He failed the English in only one way. He left no worthy heir to govern in his distinguished place.

The death of Olaf, King of Norway, at the Battle of Stiklestad in 1030, from an ancient manuscript.

Opposite *Canute rejected the pagan Viking gods, and became a Christian. In 1026, he travelled to Rome as a pilgrim to meet Pope John XIX.*

2 WHO WERE THE VIKINGS?

Above *A Viking longship travels up a fjord towards a village on its shore. The map shows the Scandinavian homeland of the Vikings — Sweden, Denmark and Norway.*

Vikings were pirates, townsmen and traders, farmers and explorers, colonizers and adventurers, and skilled craftsmen. They were also excellent sailors, some would say the most remarkable mariners in history.

The name Viking may come from '*vik*', meaning inlet. Their native Scandinavia is famous for its inlets, known as fjords. These Norwegians, Danes and Swedes were also known as Norsemen, the dreaded men of the North. They were the most northerly of the Germanic races, cousins of the Anglo-Saxons they terrorized. About the year 800, they started to expand — to erupt — overseas.

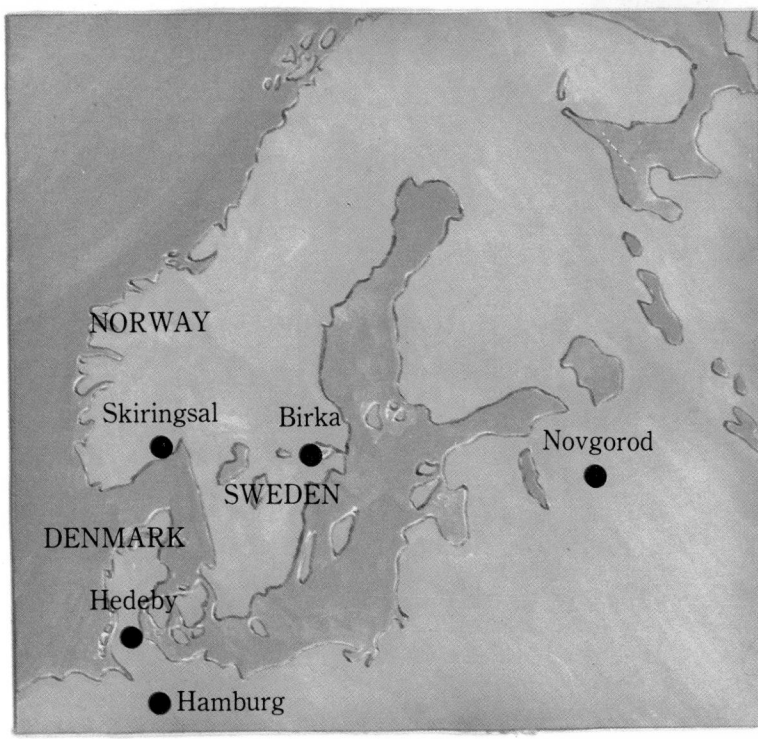

This eruption changed the history of Europe and the world. It was due to many things: love of adventure and plunder; wanderlust; and the need to find new lands because their own homeland was not fertile enough to support the rapidly growing population. They set out in 'longships' to brave the fiercest seas and reached many remote corners of the world.

Viking explorers discovered the North American continent, conquered Ireland and settled in England. They founded Normandy, colonised Russia and dominated the Mediterranean. For 300 years they were very powerful and much feared. Gradually the Vikings intermarried and blended in with other peoples. Many British people today are descended from the Vikings. The terror they caused and their horrible cruelty cannot be shrugged off. In a barbaric age, Vikings were the most brutal. Yet these same raiders rapidly turned into valuable settlers who enriched the nations in which they put down roots.

Above *The terrifying prow of a Viking longship.*

11

3 TARGET — ENGLAND!

Viking fury

On an ancient stone cross is inscribed a haunting, fear-provoking prayer: 'From the fury of the Norsemen, good Lord deliver us!' Danish Vikings were the chief scourges of England. They were helped by the Norwegians who colonised northern Scotland and the Orkneys. The Swedes cut deep into Russia, mainly as traders.

The British Isles were the chief victims of Norse fury. They were geographically nearby and were split into many factions. Experts have unearthed Viking settlements in the Orkney and Shetland islands which date back to the late eighth and early ninth centuries.

The invaders enter English history with a small landing at Portland in Dorset, then part of Wessex, in 789. Three shiploads of Vikings landed. They killed a magistrate and his men, the magistrate having mistaken them for harmless traders.

Serious attacks started in 793 when the monastery of Lindisfarne on Holy Island off the Northumbrian coast was assaulted. The raiders killed some monks and carried off others to sell as slaves. They also stole the monastery's famous collection of gold and jewels. News of the atrocity rang round Christian Europe.

The attacks on England multiplied as the Vikings sailed their shallow longships up the rivers of the east coast into the heart of the country. The Saxon kingdoms of England were no match for the invading Danes. Under great leaders like Ragnar Lothbrok, or Leather-Breeches, and Ivar the Boneless it seemed that the Vikings had all England at their mercy.

Opposite *Viking raiders plunder the monastery of Lindisfarne in 793.*

Above *This ancient stone from Gotland in Sweden shows a ship full of Viking warriors.*

Above *The Lindisfarne Stone might have been carved to remember the Viking raid on Lindisfarne in 793.*

Above *The Alfred Jewel has the words 'Alfred had me made' around its edge.*

A piece of text from the Treaty of Chippenham between Alfred and Guthrum.

Wessex stands firm

England in the 9th century was split into many kingdoms. The Vikings controlled the north and west, including the important kingdoms of Mercia: the Saxons clung on to Wessex. The steamroller progress of the Vikings was halted when the hard-pressed Saxons found a dynamic new leader in Alfred.

In Alfred's time, Viking raids on England began in earnest. In 871 it seemed that Wessex, like other English kingdoms, must fall to the Vikings. But at Ashdown in Berkshire, Alfred defeated the Danish Vikings by leading his Wessex men, 'like a wild boar', to a great victory.

Alfred became King of Wessex in the same year, on the death of his brother, Ethelred I. To gain time, he bought off the money-loving Danes. There was an uneasy truce which did not last long. On Twelfth Night in 878, Alfred was peacefully celebrating at Chippenham in Wiltshire.

That night, the Danes launched a surprise attack. Alfred fled to the forested swamps of the Isle of Athelney in Somerset. If captured he would have suffered the 'blood eagle', like other captured kings. His ribs and lungs would have been cut from him while still alive, then spread like eagle's wings in honour of the Viking god Odin.

Alfred gathered a new army together. In 878 he defeated the Danes under Guthrum at Edington in Wiltshire. Instead of killing his prisoners, he had them baptised into the Christian faith. Alfred had saved the south and west from the Viking menace. At the Treaty of Chippenham, he forced Guthrum to swear to leave Wessex in peace. If Alfred had been killed, the Vikings would have ruled the whole island and it is possible that the English-speaking world would not now exist.

Opposite *Alfred, disguised as a minstrel, sings to the Viking leader, Guthrum, hoping to find out what plans the Vikings had for attacking his Saxon people.*

Stalemate

Seven years of tranquillity followed the Treaty of Chippenham. Then, in 885, a new wave of Vikings from overseas ravaged the north coast of Kent, besieging the city of Rochester. Alfred beat off the attack and occupied London. His triumph was short-lived and throughout the first half of the 890s, the Saxons were harried by the 'Great Army' of Vikings.

Further attacks bore down upon Kent and the West Country. In Kent, a fleet of 250 ships sailed inland and wrecked one of Alfred's 'burhs', or townships. After years of slaughter, fierce fighting and the death of the greatest warriors on both sides, a stalemate was reached. The Anglo-Saxon Chronicle (a history of England started in the reign of Alfred) was able to report in 896 that, 'by the grace of God, the army had not on the whole afflicted the English people very greatly'. By the time of Alfred's death in 899, the south and west of England were safe, but the territory to the north, known as the Danelaw, was firmly under Viking control.

In fact, England, apart from Wessex and Kent, was now Anglo-Danish with Viking and Saxon living side by side, and even intermarrying. There is plenty of evidence of Viking settlement in the Danelaw. Archaeologists have uncovered Viking remains in at least five important cities — Nottingham, Leicester, Derby, Lincoln and York. York — Jorvik to the Vikings — was one of the greatest Viking centres of the age. Place names also bear witness to Viking colonisation in England. For example, all place names ending in -by (a farm or a village), -thwaite (a meadow), and -thorpe (a village) are Scandinavian in origin.

A stone cross found in York showing a tenth century Viking landowner.

Opposite *The map shows the division of England during the ninth and tenth centuries into the Danelaw — the area controlled by the Vikings — and Wessex, still under Saxon control.*

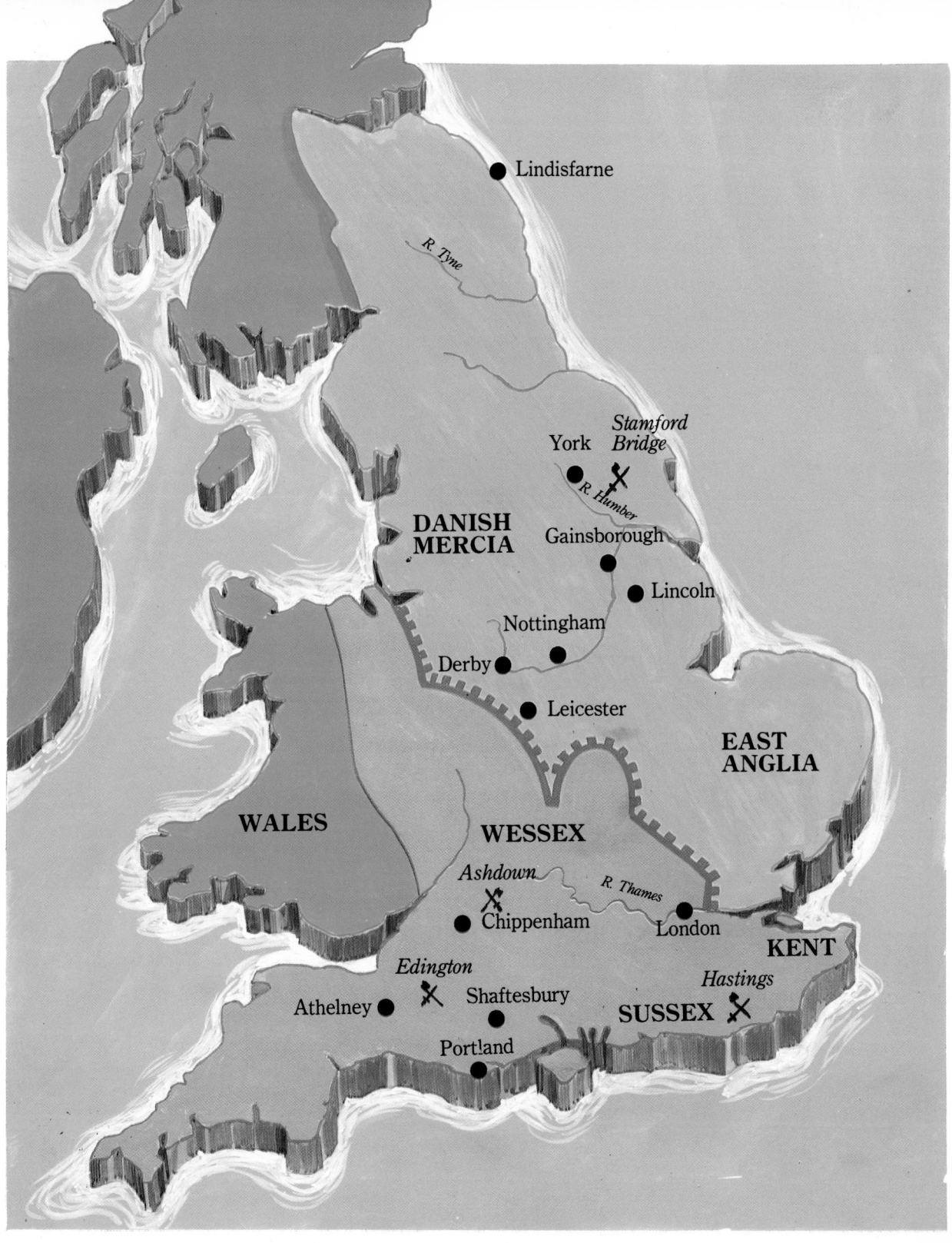

Lindisfarne

R. Tyne

York *Stamford Bridge*

R. Humber

DANISH MERCIA

Gainsborough

Lincoln

Nottingham

Derby

Leicester

EAST ANGLIA

WALES

WESSEX

Ashdown

R. Thames

Chippenham

London

KENT

Edington

Hastings

Athelney

Shaftesbury

SUSSEX

Portland

Vikings in retreat

The Vikings now found themselves opposed by Alfred's successors, a formidable line of Saxon kings. A Danish army under King Eric of East Anglia was defeated by Alfred's son, Edward the Elder, in 910. By 917, the Vikings had lost all of the Danelaw south of the River Humber. The Danes were allowed to remain, and they were forced to recognise Edward as ruler of all England. Even the princes of Wales accepted him as overlord.

In 937, the Vikings struck back. The Viking King Olaf of Dublin, Vikings from Norway, and Constantine, King of the Scots, joined forces to destroy Edward's son, King Athelstan. The invaders were met by Athelstan who had gathered an army of Englishmen and a few second generation Danish settlers. A great battle was fought at Brunanburh in 937, an unknown spot, somewhere in the north of England. The Viking invaders were utterly routed, five of their kings and seven earls perishing in the slaughter.

It was a stunning blow to the Vikings. For the next few years they were kept on the defensive, first by Athelstan, then by his half-brothers Edmund and Edred and finally by the brilliant King Edgar. One attempt at rebellion in Northumbria, led by a ferocious Viking named Eric 'Bloodaxe', was crushed. Otherwise, the Vikings were subdued and, under Edgar, Saxons and Vikings lived together in harmony. But could it last?

Above *Athelstan's Saxon army routs the Vikings at the Battle of Brunanburh.*

Left *Three silver pennies from the Viking kingdom of York.*

Right *Viking weapons — a sword, two axe-heads and a spearhead.*

New Raids

Above *A bronze weathervane from a longship.*

In the 980s, the Vikings were attacking England once again. King Edgar had died in 975, aged only 32. His 15-year-old son Edward was murdered, probably by supporters of his half-brother, Ethelred the Unready, who became king. The Vikings were encouraged by Ethelred's weakness to renew their forays.

England was very wealthy at that time, so the Vikings — driven by greed above all — made easy money. Ethelred tried to keep them at bay by paying them Danegeld. Some of that wealth has since been discovered in Scandinavia where much of the loot was taken. Ethelred would have benefitted from the advice offered by the poet, Rudyard Kipling, nearly 1,000 years later:

> If once you have paid him the Danegeld
> You never get rid of the Dane.

Vikings attacked local Saxon leaders, such as the brave Earl Brihtnoth. Before giving battle, the Vikings called upon Brihtnoth to 'send treasure quickly in return for peace', and advised him that 'it is better for you to buy off an attack with tribute than to fight with men as fierce as we are'. They were true words as Brihtnoth discovered to his cost, for he was killed and his troops cut to pieces at the Battle of Maldon in 991.

In 1009, a Norwegian Viking, Olaf the Stout, destroyed London Bridge so that he could sail further up the River Thames. This tumultuous event gave rise to the old nursery rhyme, 'London Bridge is falling down'. But Ethelred's cruellest opponent was Swein Forkbeard, who waged a constant war against his disintegrating kingdom. By 1014, Ethelred had lost England to the Vikings. Two years later, England was in Canute's firm grip.

A coin minted in the reign of Ethelred the Unready.

Opposite *Olaf the Stout's longship pulls down London Bridge.*

A Viking peace

It is difficult to know what it was like to be an Englishman or a Dane in Canute's England, for written sources are few. Yet there can be little doubt that Canute gave his new kingdom their first taste of peace for a quarter of a century, enabling Saxon and Viking to live contentedly together.

Danegeld had crippled England's finances, so Canute had to introduce some stern financial measures. Taxation was high, the money going to improve England's shattered defences. Canute rewarded his followers for their services and a number of estates passed into Danish hands. He used mostly Danish officials to help him govern. Yet by giving his people the priceless gift of peace most Saxons must have become reconciled to Danish rule. The ferocious Viking raider became almost more of an Englishman than the English themselves.

After Canute's death in 1035, his unworthy son Harthacnut succeeded him, but after two years of poor rule, he died unexpectedly at a wedding feast. There was a scrabble for power until the English elected as their king, the son of Ethelred the Unready and Emma of Normandy, Edward the Confessor (1042-1066).

Edward's saintly manner led to his nickname, the Confessor. A power struggle developed between Edward and his Norman advisers, and the powerful Godwin family. It was to lead to a succession crisis on Edward's death in 1066. Harold Godwinson and William, Duke of Normandy, each believed he should be king. But, because of the Canute connection, the Vikings had their own claims to the English throne. The countdown to the last days of Anglo-Danish England had begun.

Above *A sturdy Viking pail used for fetching water.*

A coin from the reign of Edward the Confessor.

Opposite *During Canute's reign, Saxon and Viking lived contentedly together. Here a Viking draws water from a pond for a Saxon lady.*

Last of the Vikings

The last great Viking to try to seize the English throne was one of the most famous warriors of the age, the giant King Harald Hardrada of Norway. Others were after the same prize. William of Normandy believed it was his. Yet when Edward the Confessor died in 1066, the Crown went to Harold Godwinson who had earlier sworn over sacred relics to support William's claim. William prepared to invade England. So did Hardrada.

The Viking's claim was not strong, but that did not deter him. He had an unexpected ally in Tostig, King Harold of England's brother. He had been driven out of Northumbria for his bad rule and was enraged because his brother had not supported him. Now he wanted revenge.

Harald Hardrada and Tostig joined forces in Scotland, then sailed south with a big Viking fleet. William's

Above *A twelfth-century chessman depicts a Viking warrior.*

invasion force was held up by the winds that blew the other invaders south. Hardrada reached the River Tyne with 300 ships. Cleveland was attacked and Scarborough sacked, before the Viking army set up a base at Riccall. Soon the great Viking king was master of York, having scattered English troops.

Meanwhile King Harold of England raced north, picking up troops as he marched. On 25th September, he came upon them at Stamford Bridge near York. A single Viking tried to hold the bridge over the River Derwent after his comrades had fallen. When he too was killed, the English poured across and annihilated the invaders. Hardrada was killed by an arrow in his throat and Tostig, too, died. It was one of the worst defeats the Vikings had ever suffered. On 14th October 1066, Harold of England was killed at the Battle of Hastings, defeated by William of Normandy, himself of Viking descent.

Below *English soldiers watch the Viking fleet carrying Harald Hardrada's invasion force as it approaches the coast.*

4 VIKING EXPLORATION

The longship

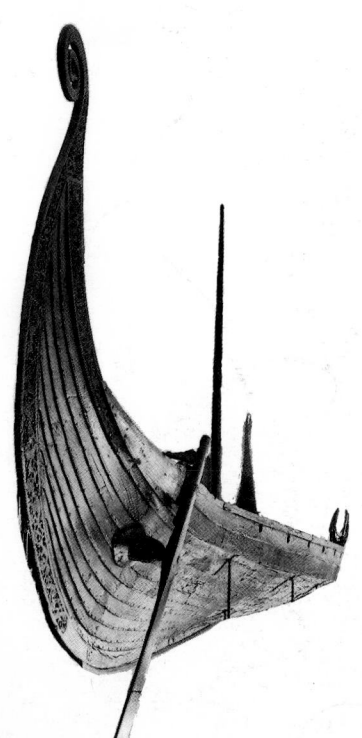

The longship discovered during excavations at Oseberg.

The Vikings' power was due, above all, to two things — their fighting prowess and their superb longships. By the end of the ninth century, when their days of blood-drenched glory were at their height, they had perfected these marvellous vessels.

Kings were buried in their ships for use in the next world and some have been dug up, almost in tact. We therefore know a great deal about them. This world has rarely seen more perfect vessels.

Beautiful to look at, they carried Vikings as far as North America and deep into the heart of Russia. The longship had such a shallow draught that it could reach far up the rivers of Europe, increasing its range of terror and trade.

The longship had a single sail, usually colourfully striped, and when a longship entered port the warriors' shields were displayed on the sides. The vessels were clinker-built, meaning they had overlapping planks. The hull was therefore flexible enough to give against the waves, and stormy seas presented no problems. Rope was put in the joints to make them watertight. At the stern and bows there were often ferocious carved figures to scare evil spirits away. They must have scared the Vikings' enemies, too.

These ships could hold up to 200 men, Viking flagships holding some 300. There were also smaller and broader merchant ships called knarrs. As Sir Winston Churchill truthfully wrote, 'The soul of the Viking lay in the longships'.

Opposite *Viking craftsmen work hard to produce another longship.*

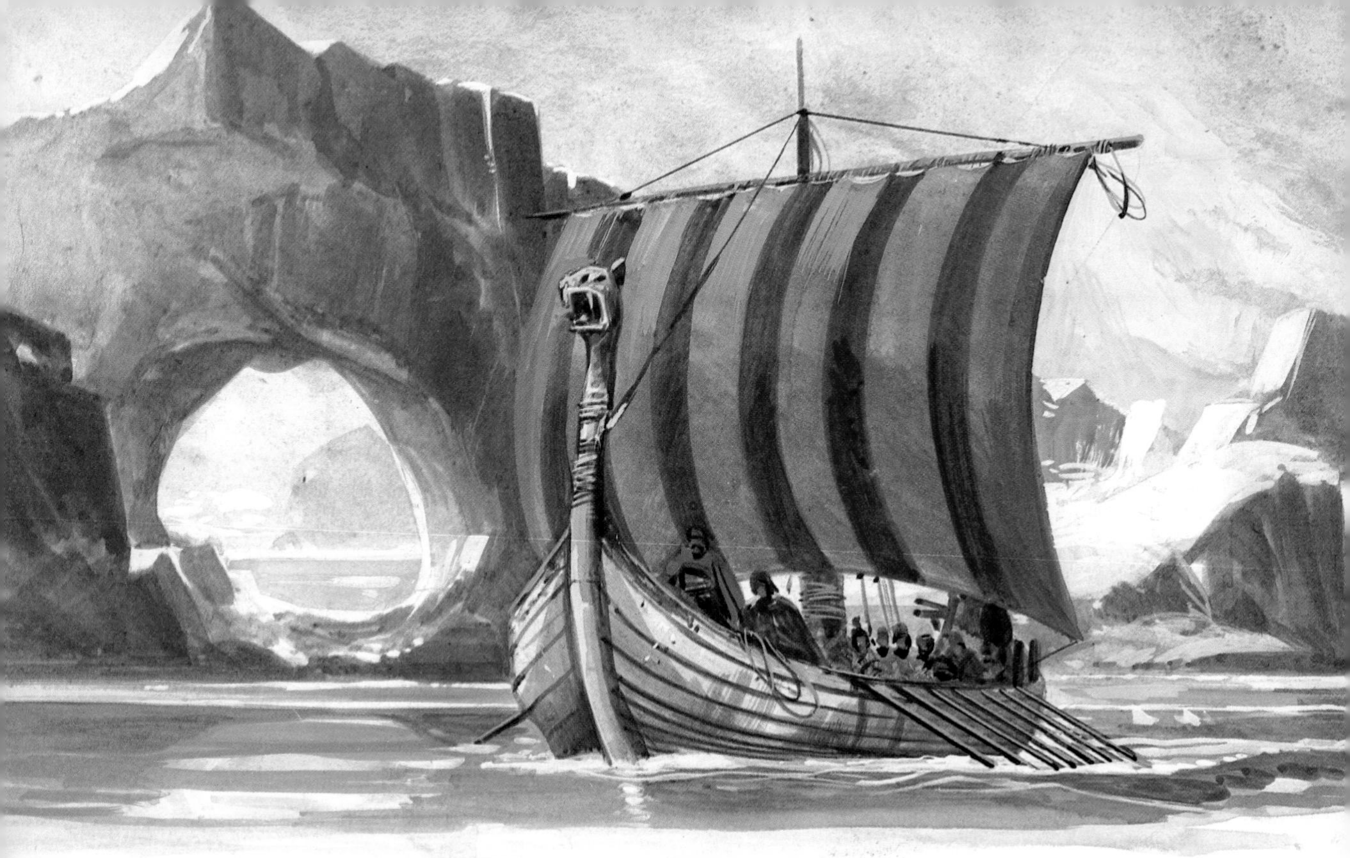

Above *Eric the Red's longship sails through the icy waters off Greenland.*

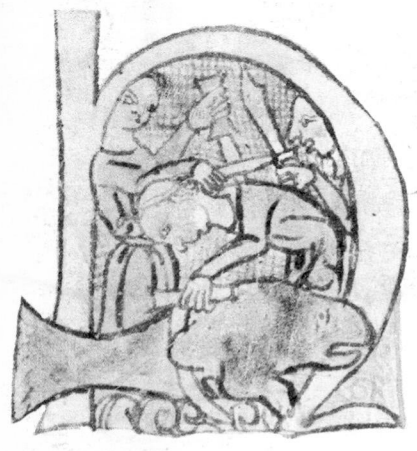

Vikings in Iceland cut the blubber from a beached whale, (from a fourteenth century book).

America discovered

Viking sagas are full of voyages of discovery to the 'New World', almost 500 years before Columbus 'discovered' it in 1492. We cannot be sure that they are true, but it is claimed that a Viking settlement, unearthed on Newfoundland in 1962, dates back to 1000, so there might well be some substance to the story.

Sailing west, the Vikings made some important discoveries. About 860, a Norwegian Viking named Naddod set out with his men and was driven by a storm to an island, which he called Snowland — today's Iceland. Not liking what they saw, he and his men, who had been blown off course from the Faeroe Islands, sailed away.

A Swedish Viking, Gardar Svavarsson, was also driven by a storm to Iceland about the same time. He explored the coastline properly. Another Viking, Floki

Vilgerdarson, followed him and started a colony, giving the island its name. Conditions were harsh for the colonists, but by 920 there were some 20,000 people in Iceland and 60,000 by the next century. They found a freedom there that they had lacked at home.

Next came Greenland, explored in 982 by the outlaw Erik the Red, so-called because of his flaming hair and beard. When Erik reached the country, he found a few patches of green grass, so he named it Greenland to encourage Vikings to go and live there. Life was rugged, the winters severe, but farming was possible.

It was Erik's son Leif who, it is claimed, discovered the New World, though there were tales of a new land seen by Bjarni Thordarson in 986. Leif landed at Helluland (Baffin Island), Markland (Labrador) and Vinland (Newfoundland). Leif and his men spent a few winters there before hostility from 'Skraelings' — Eskimos or Indians — forced the settlers to return to Greenland.

Below *A map showing Viking exploration in the North Atlantic.*

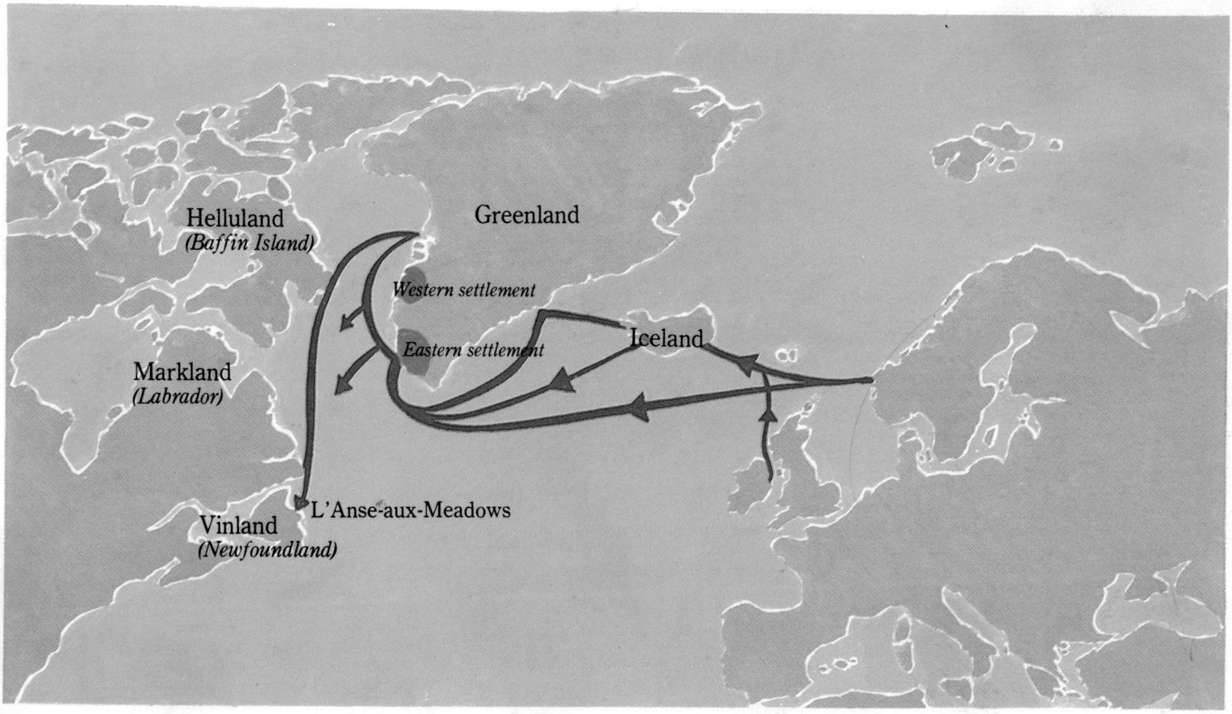

Helluland
(Baffin Island)

Greenland

Western settlement

Eastern settlement

Iceland

Markland
(Labrador)

L'Anse-aux-Meadows

Vinland
(Newfoundland)

Europe overrun

While the British Isles were being harassed, other bands of Vikings were stealing up the rivers of Europe. They cut deep into the heartland of France. To a writer at the time, the flood of Vikings seemed never-ending.

The city of Nantes was put to the sword in 843. Moorish kingdoms in Spain were under attack. Parts of Italy were assailed. At first, Christian Europe could deal with the threat, especially if the Vikings could be brought to a pitched battle, but things changed.

Year after year the assaults on France increased. The closer French towns were to rivers the greater the chance of disaster. In 885 the invaders, led by Siegfried, besieged Paris. The French king, Charles the Fat, paid the Vikings a fortune in Danegeld to persuade them to keep away.

Taxes spiralled to raise the money. Monasteries were abandoned and some cities like Orleans were attacked so often that they virtually ceased to exist.

Finally, in 911, a Viking marauder called Rolf made a treaty with the French king, Charles the Simple, which gave him the Duchy of Normandy. Soon Rolf, now Rollo, was rebuilding the churches that he and his men had destroyed. Before long the fierce piratical Vikings became fierce, but less piratical, Normans. The Viking skill of adapting to their new homelands was remarkable.

Yet memories of the Viking terror must have lingered on. Cities had been sacked from the River Rhine to the River Seine. At their terrible worst it must have seemed that the Vikings were bringing about the end of the world.

Viking raiders besiege Paris in 885 as part of a campaign of terror against France.

31

The founding of Russia

The Vikings had to drag their longships overland between rivers as they explored deep into the heart of Russia.

It was Swedish Vikings who headed eastwards to what is now Russia, seeking, as always, adventure and plunder. They took their longships down the Volga, Dvina and Dnieper rivers and used slaves to drag them overland in the portage stages between rivers. They met Slavic tribes who, like so many other peoples, were no match for the invaders. In fact it is sometimes said that the Slavs were so impressed by the Vikings that the wild rovers were invited to stay, to prevent their own tribes from fighting. They called them 'Rus', the origin of the name Russia. Tradition has it that the Slavs invited a Viking leader named Rurik to settle in Novgorod in 862. He is reputed to be the founder of Russia.

Other Vikings travelled far across the great continent. Some reached Baghdad, now the capital of Iraq. Others

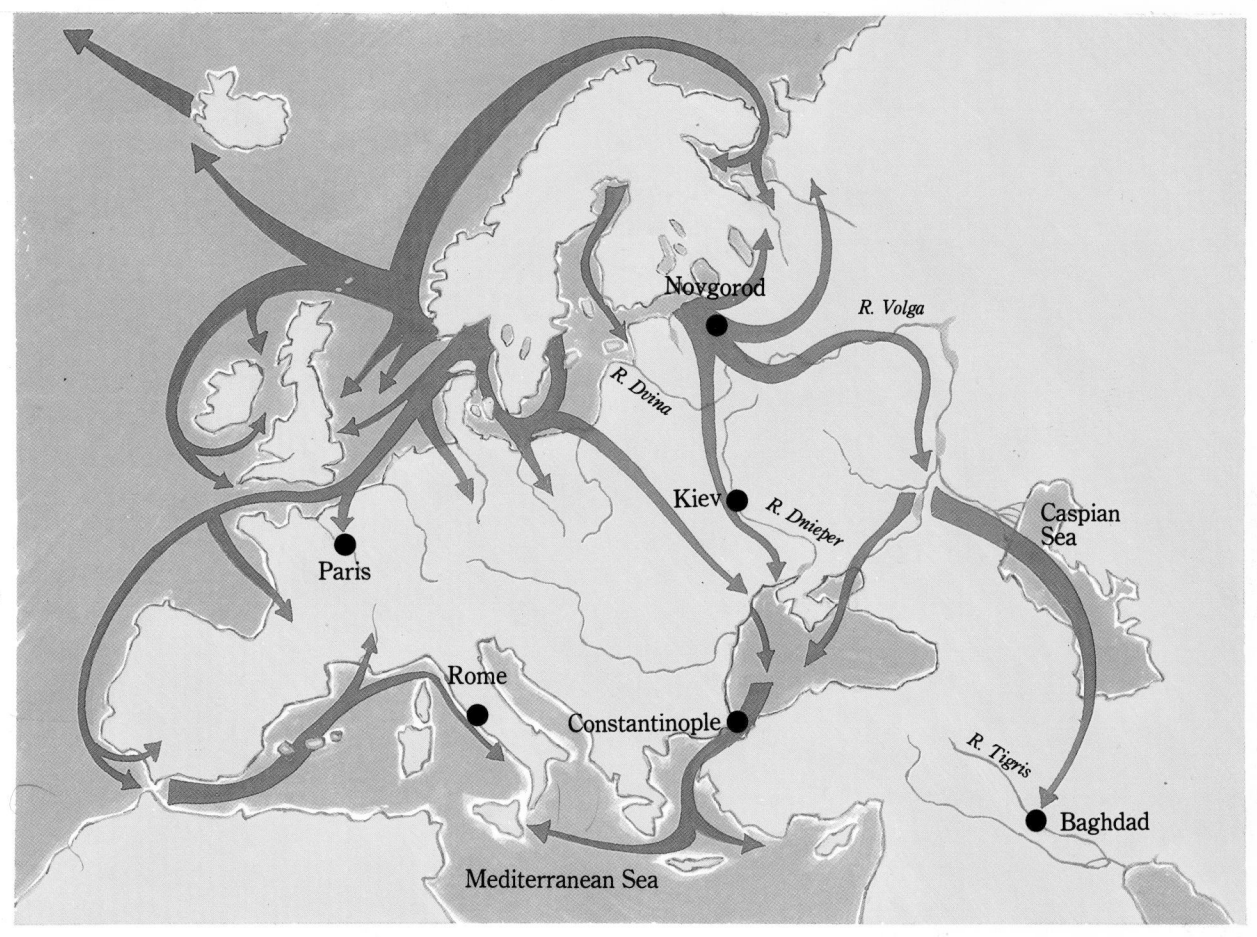

Labels on map: Novgorod, R. Volga, R. Dvina, Kiev, R. Dnieper, Caspian Sea, Paris, Rome, Constantinople, R. Tigris, Baghdad, Mediterranean Sea

opened up a lively trade with the Byzantine Emperor in Constantinople from a trading base in the great city of Kiev. The change from a stark Scandinavian hut to the luxury of the Orient, must have startled Viking warriors — but their astonishment soon turned to delight.

So astonishing was the Norse talent for switching from savage warfare to profitable trading that Viking strongholds rapidly became market towns. Apart from plentiful animal skins and slaves, the Vikings found hordes of silver, one of their greatest loves. In many places across the continent, archaeologists have discovered caches of silver buried by the Vikings which prove the vast extent of Viking conquest and trade.

A map showing the extent of Viking exploration and trading throughout the European continent.

Moorish traders brought slaves to sell in the booming market towns of Scandinavia.

5 EVERYDAY LIFE

Viking traders

Say the word 'Viking' and most people will think of a warrior, of plunder and longships. Yet the Vikings were great traders as well and it was the search for trade that led them to explore many new lands.

That the Vikings valued trade is shown in 845 when a strong band of warriors attacked the trading port of Hamburg close to the mouth of the River Elbe. These Danish Vikings devastated the city but did not harm the large merchant quarter, full of shops and houses, which lay undefended outside the city walls.

Many Vikings travelled far to the market towns of Birka in Sweden and Skiringsal in Norway. But the most famous of all their trading towns was Hedeby in Denmark where, 'more people go than to any other place in the North while the fair lasts'. True it seems to have been too noisy for a Moorish trader who visited it in the 10th century and complained about animal sacrifices hanging on poles outside houses, and everyone eating fish. Yet traders would come all the way from Spain and Africa to buy jewellery, glass, cloth — and slaves, the wretched victims of Viking raids.

The town was well sited for traders and could be easily defended. But it could not stand up to Harold Hardrada of Norway. During an inter-Viking war with the Danes in 1050, he burnt the great market town to the ground.

Below *Tenth-century folding scales, pan and lead weights recently discovered in York.*

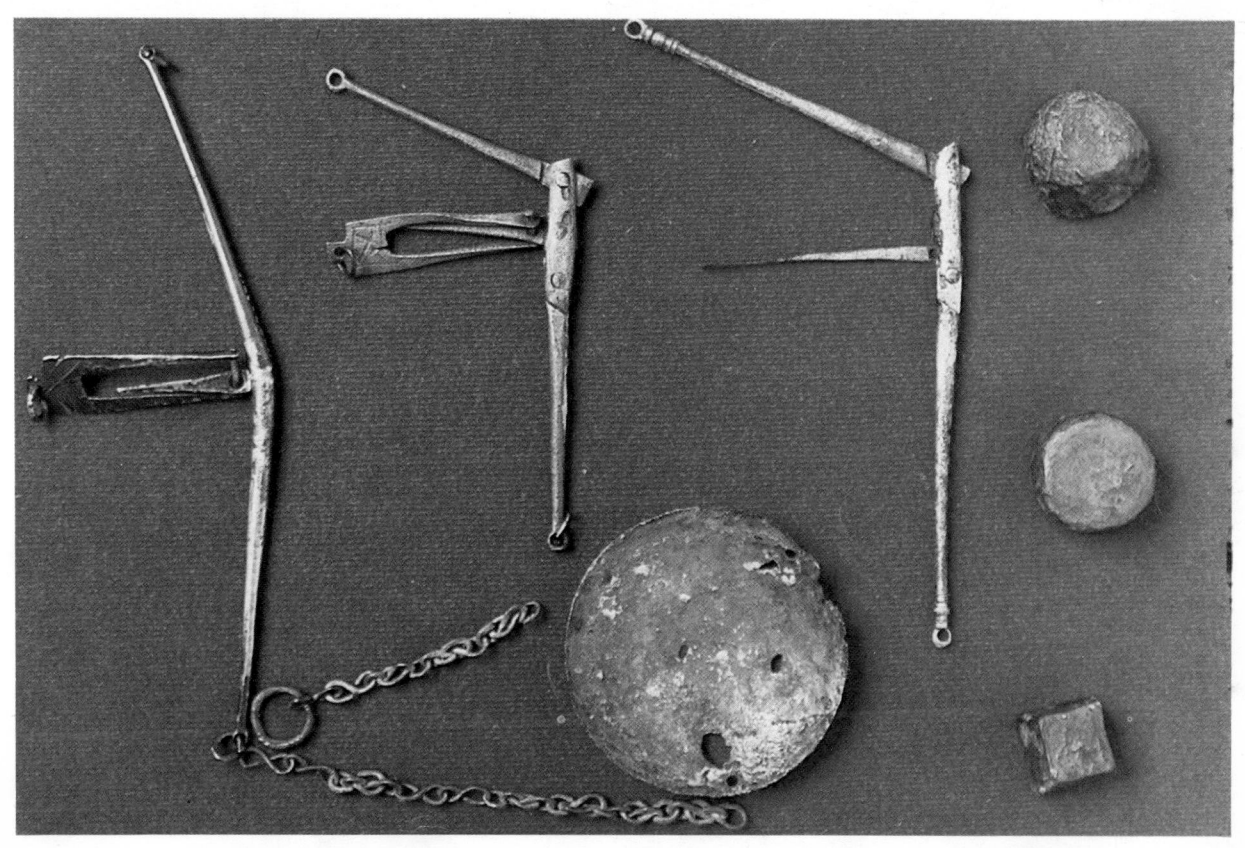

In the stifling heat of a forge, a blacksmith fashions the blade of a sword.

Town life

The Vikings were a great trading people who built many towns as centres for trade. People travelled for miles to sell their goods. They needed places to stay, eat and show the goods they had to offer. Towns grew up in response to their needs.

As recent excavations have shown, York was an important town in Viking times, which carried on a lively trade. A ship docking at York on the banks of the River Ouse might be carrying skins, wine, furs, amber, pottery and other goods. They would leave well-stocked with jewellery, leather and slaves. Plenty of coins have been

A delicate silver ear-ring found in Russia.

excavated to prove that money often changed hands in these trading transactions. Think of Vikings trying on shoes, making padlocks and excellent scales.

Hedeby in Denmark was a great market town. Birka in Sweden was a veritable boom town, controlling the fur trade to the north and boasting an important market-place. Viking towns were most likely to be sited on rivers. Defence was very important. Birka had a nightmarish approach to it from the Baltic Sea, and the risk of attack was lessened even more by high ground above it, a lake and man-made fortifications.

The Viking world was not divided into traders and warriors. Some were both. A man who had been slaughtering and pillaging a month earlier might be found in the market-place getting a good price for his loot.

The Saxons had towns and Alfred was a noted town planner, but the Vikings seemed to be as happy in towns as they were setting out for a raid.

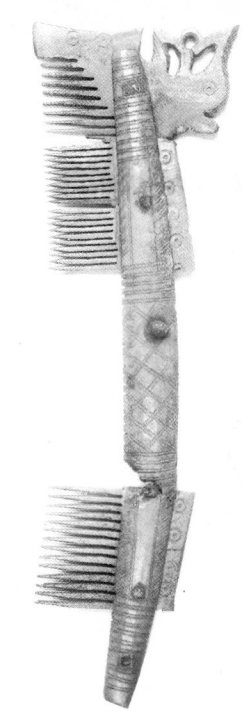

Below *An assortment of tools used by Viking craftsmen.*

Above *A Viking bone comb.*

Country life

For all the Vikings' love of trading and therefore town life, they were mostly country folk, their lives governed by the seasons of the year. It was not an easy life for the Scandinavian farmer, for much of the soil was poor and needed extra hard work to produce the necessities of life like corn and other crops. The soil of the British Isles, expecially England and Ireland, must have delighted the raiders turned settlers.

Cattle were very important to Viking families. They grazed in the richer pastures of the hills and mountains in the summer. Butter and cheese were important items of diet, while animals slaughtered in the autumn would see the family through the harsh northern winters.

In the countryside, Vikings were divided into three classes. The lowest class was the 'thrall' (slave), used as little more than a beast of burden. Their lives were a

The foundations of a Viking farmhouse at Jarlshof on the Shetland Islands.

continuous round of sweated labour to build fences, till the ground and herd livestock. Next came the 'karl' (farmer) who was in charge of his farm labourers and built ploughs, carts and houses. At the top was the 'Jarl' (chieftain) who, 'waged war, reddening the battlefield with blood and killing the damned' as well as more innocent pursuits like playing dice and swimming. Women were in a class of their own, looking after cattle as well as busying themselves with domestic chores which included taking the lice out of their husband's hair!

Viking women did not just stay in and look after the home. When their husbands went raiding, they looked after the cattle and did many other jobs.

Above *A Viking tells stories of his adventures to his children.*

Two leather shoes recently unearthed at York.

Home life

The main Viking house was a long house, whose thick walls were made from timber or wattle and daub. Some had roofs of turf which went right down to the ground. Others were covered with wooden shingles or thatch.

A typical Viking house had a single room where the family lived and ate. Animals might join them in harsh winter weather. Furniture was basic, with wooden benches and tables. Carpets were made from rushes and reeds. In the centre of the long house was a fire pit which belched smoke into the room and hopefully out through a small hole in the roof. Light and air came in through narrow slits in the walls, so it must have been dim and smoky inside a Viking long house. Living conditions improved down the years. From sleeping on the floor, tne family might sleep on platforms round the walls, while the head of the family might have a bed and a chair t himself.

Viking women had more freedom than the women in other parts of Europe. When the men were away for months at a time, raiding or trading, the women were in complete charge of the household. They were permitted to keep their property after a marriage. If they did not like the husband chosen for them by their father, they were usually spared the marriage. Divorce was easy if things went wrong.

Vikings of both sexes dressed in simple woollen clothes, unless a special occasion demanded something smarter. Then both men and women dyed their clothes, put make-up on their faces, wore a fine array of jewellery, and must have looked very striking.

Below *A collection of cooking utensils — a pot, bowl, jug, jar and a spit for roasting meat — used by the Vikings.*

Viking feasts

Vikings, like the Saxons, needed little excuse for having a feast. Families feasted in their long houses after the harvest and at weddings. But the biggest feasts of all took place in the chief's great hall. The lady of the house covered the tables with embroidered cloths of white linen. She then produced the food and laid it out on the table. A typical feast would consist of ham and roast meat with plenty of white bread to fill the gaps.

Despite the delicious food, eaten off wooden plates using knives and spoons, drink was the main attraction. Entertainment was provided by minstrels, horn-playing musicians, jesters and story-tellers. These wanderers would relate the dramatic sagas of past heroes, or stories of the Norse gods and goddesses. As they told their tales, ale and mead — an alcoholic drink made from honey — were consumed in vast quantities from drinking horns. These drinking horns were usually made from animal horns, but some were works of art, fashioned from silver and beautifully carved. Beakers and cups were used as well.

Feasts could last for days and called for careful preparation. They quite often took place on Thor's Day, our Thursday, but Yule in midwinter was the most important Viking feast of all.

Wrestling contests were popular at Viking feasts. The Vikings also had sauna baths, which they visited to work up a good sweat after too much eating and drinking — and then dashed outside to roll in the snow.

Opposite *On special occasions, like a wedding or the end of the harvest, Vikings feasted until they could eat and drink no more.*

Below *An ornate silver hunting horn.*

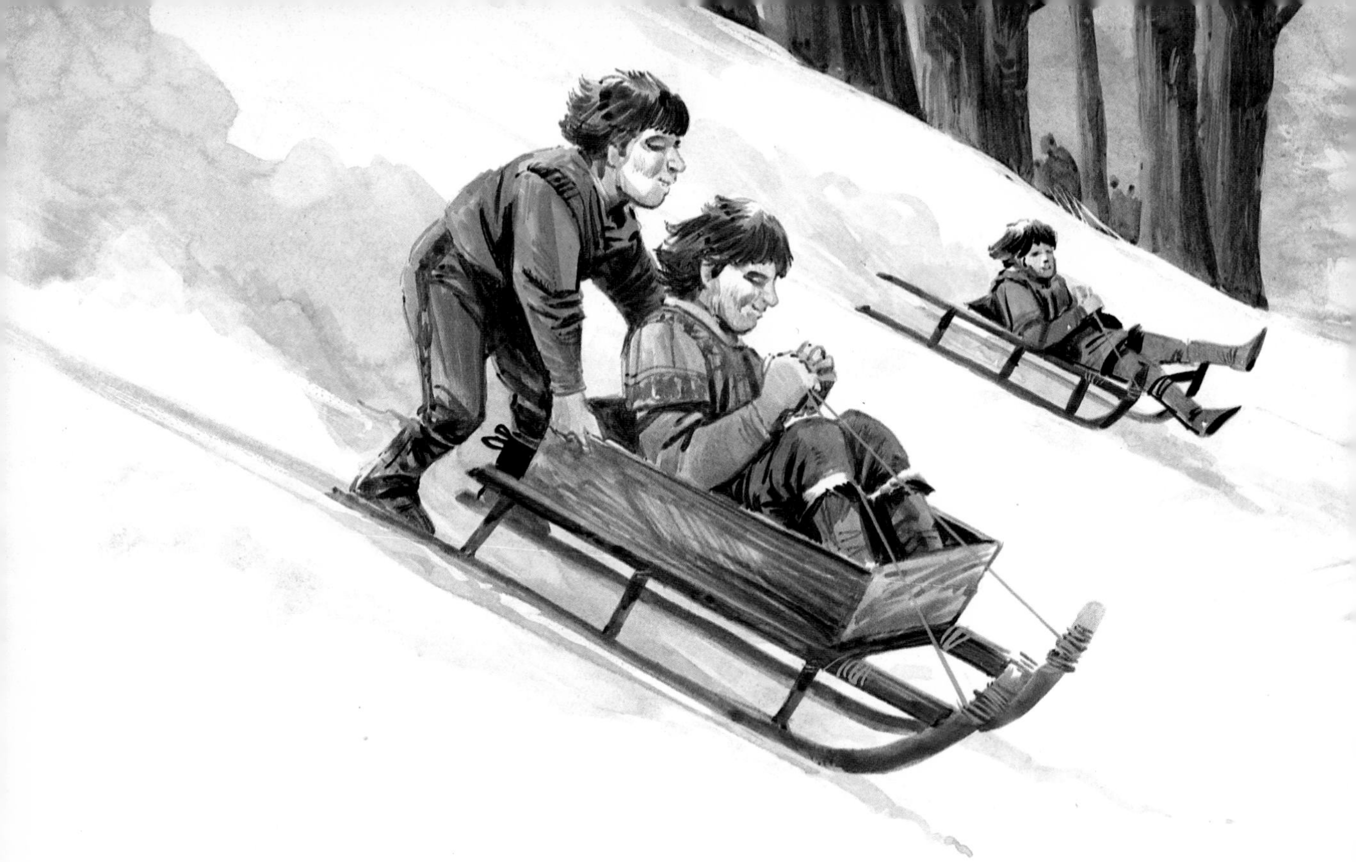

Below *A Viking chess piece made from a walrus tusk.*

Sports and entertainments

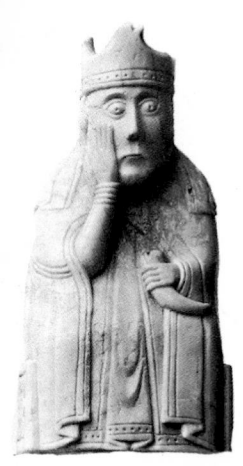

There can be no doubt that the most popular Viking sport was fighting. Fitness meant much to Vikings, and wrestling was good training for warriors. A typical Viking form of entertainment was for men to get together for trials of strength. Alas, injuries and deaths could be the result of these no-holds-barred scraps which could lead to a long-lasting blood feud between families. It comes as no surprise to learn that cowards were despised by the Vikings.

However, there were less savage sports, even though many ordinary games seem to have ended in fighting. Less lethal activities including skiing, riding in sledges,

Above *During the harsh Scandinavian winters the Vikings enjoyed sledging, and skating on bone skates.*

Below *Viking pipes made from bones.*

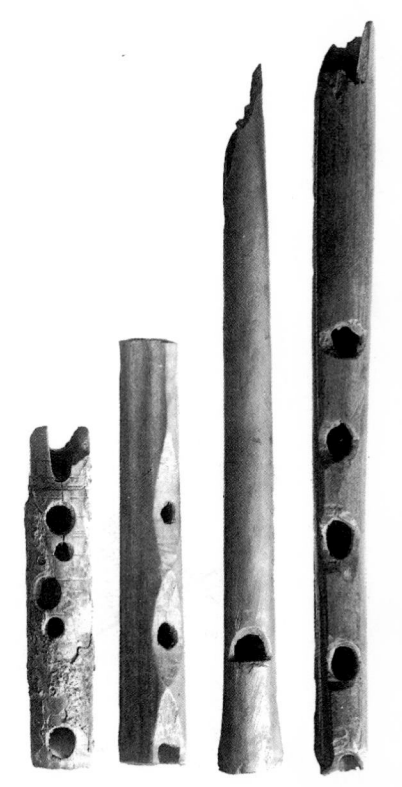

swimming and ball games. Horses were used, not just for riding but for stallion-fighting, a savage form of sport which often resulted in the death of one of the combatants. The Vikings believed that their crops would grow better if the stallions put on a brave show.

Music was popular, especially as part of feasts, and storytelling was always welcome entertainment. The Vikings had their own form of a chess-like game, using pieces made of walrus ivory. Some have survived to this day. There was also a game similar to draughts. Weddings could provide much entertainment, one wedding feast being on record as lasting an entire month!

A Viking craftsman carves a dragon's head for the prow of a longship.

Arts and crafts

Vikings were vain and proud of their appearance. They loved jewellery and when they went raiding made a point of stealing as much of it as they could lay their hands on. The loot from monasteries in early Viking raids must have been some of the richest plunder in history.

Both sexes wore well-made brooches, rings and other ornaments of silver, gold or bronze. Viking smiths were as expert at making jewellery as they were at fashioning highly decorated war axes and other weapons. Some of their weapons and helmets — which did not have horns as is sometimes believed — now rank as prized works of art, proudly displayed in museums.

The Vikings were great craftsmen in wood, proof being found when the famous Oseberg ship was discovered in Norway in 1904. It was filled with fine artefacts including a beautiful wagon with glimpses of Norse myths carved on its sides. For pure craftsmanship, the Viking longship must rank supreme.

Skinners were important people who made fine leather clothes. Like all Viking craftsmen they used as wide a range of tools as any modern craftsmen working without powered tools.

Above *A silver Viking ear-ring found in Russia.*

Left *Beautiful disc-brooches fashioned in gold.*

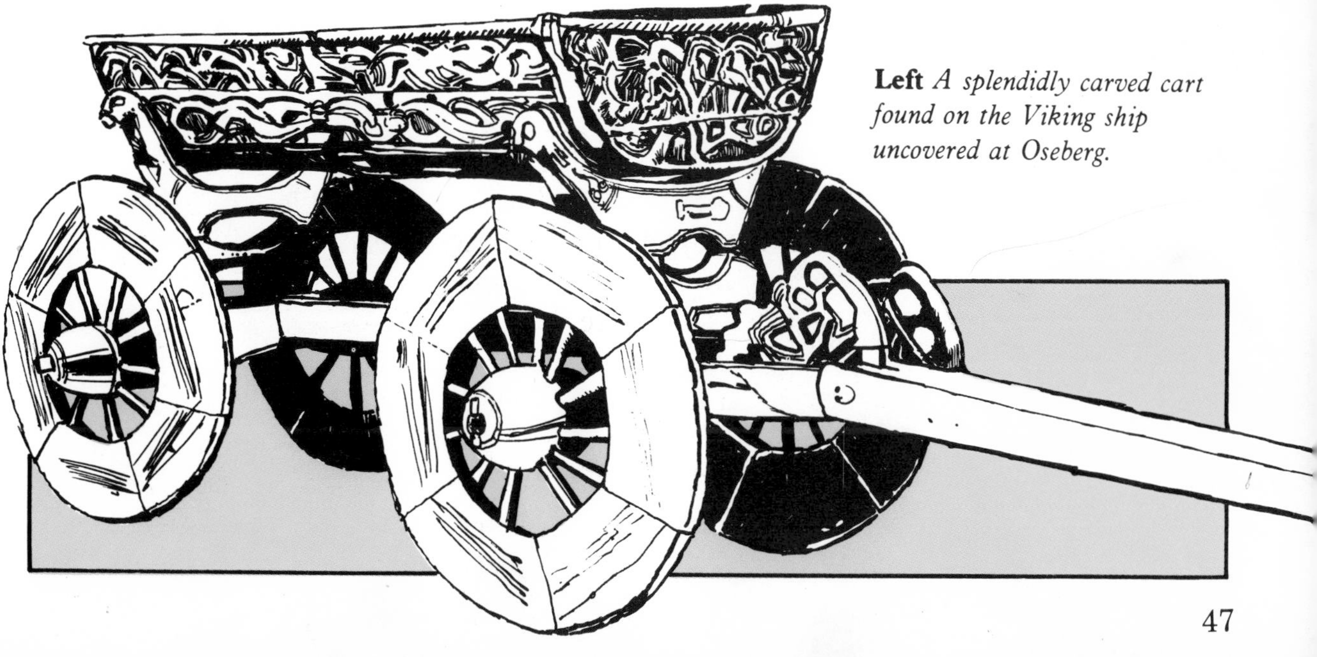

Left *A splendidly carved cart found on the Viking ship uncovered at Oseberg.*

6 HEATHEN VIKINGS

Pagan gods

Before the Vikings became Christians they worshipped a fascinating array of gods and goddesses, some of whose lives were like outsize versions of their own. There was no need for a warrior to fear death in battle, for he would instantly go to see Odin, greatest of Norse gods, and would live and feast with other heroes in the Viking heaven, Valhalla.

Like mortals, the gods were born, died, loved, fought, and were betrayed. Odin was the one-eyed god of wisdom, having sacrificed an eye to get it. His Anglo-Saxon name, Woden, has given us Wednesday. His brother Loki was the fire god and a troublemaker. Thor ruled the winds and rains and fought wicked giants with lightning flashing down from his hammer. Thunder was the sound of his chariot wheels crashing across the sky.

The most famous goddess was the beautiful Freya, goddess of love. Her brother Frey was the god of fertility who had a collapsible boat that could be fitted into a pouch or hold all the gods! There were no Viking churches except the great outdoors, where evil spirits could not harm them. These Viking gods were the ones the Saxons worshipped before becoming Christians, though under slightly different names. The Norse gods are still famous through stories, music and art. A 19th century musician called Richard Wagner wrote a famous opera called 'The Valkyries', the name given to Odin's nine daughters who took warriors to Valhalla. Norse gods are part of Europe's heritage.

Above *A silver pendant in the shape of Thor's hammer.*

Above *A bronze figure of Thor, found in Iceland.*

Opposite *Thor, the Viking god of Thunder, in his chariot, unleashing thunderbolts at his enemies.*

Sagas and legends

The Norse gods had many exciting legends told about them, and Vikings of all ages also thrilled to sagas about past heroes. Most of these sagas were passed down by word of mouth, which means that the sagas are a mixture of fact and fiction. True the Vikings had a form of writing called 'runes', magical letters said to have been a gift from Odin. But this small alphabet, 24 letters at first, then 16, was only used on gravestones; on charms worn to stave off evil; and on weapons and road markers. Not much history can be carved into such things.

The sagas were written down too long after the events

they describe ever to be considered reliable as history. Yet they are filled with useful information about the Vikings, from Icelandic families to Norwegian kings. From them we know much about Vikings in peace and war, how they traded and explored. For instance, we can learn much about the great 10th century Viking warrior, Eric 'Bloodaxe', from sagas written down long after his death, while the Vinland sagas tell the colourful story of Viking exploration in North America.

Viking legends often tell the story of kingdoms like today's Heaven and hell. We have seen that those who died in battle went straight to Valhalla. The rest were less lucky, going down to a land of snow and mists called Niflheim. This dismal belief led some to ask their friends to kill them so as to avoid Niflheim. Such is the power of myths and legends!

Ghostly figures haunt Niflheim — the icy Viking underworld.

7 THE END OF THE VIKING WORLD

The Viking world collapses

A detail from a golden altar-piece showing Harald Bluetooth's baptism by Poppo the priest.

The Battle of Hastings in 1066 sounded the death-knell for Viking power in England. Elsewhere in Europe, Viking power and influence was declining. The coming of Christianity to Scandinavia had calmed the more savage elements in the Norse character.

Denmark, led by King Harald Bluetooth (945-985), was the first country to be converted to Christianity. The story is told of how a priest called Poppo appeared before King Harald. To prove the power of Christ, Poppo picked up a red-hot iron bar which caused him no pain and did not burn his hands. Harald was so amazed that he and his followers became Christians. Norway soon

followed and then, eventually, Sweden.

There were other reasons for the decline in Viking influence. Their enemies grew stronger and were better equipped to fight off the last bands of Viking marauders. Even the Irish, who had suffered so much at the hands of the Vikings, were strong enough to defeat them at the Battle of Clontarf in 1014. Also, many of the Vikings who had gone overseas had found comfortable and prosperous homes. Viking warriors married local girls and were gradually absorbed by the native populations.

The Vikings had found that they had pushed their sphere of influence to its limit. Having reached as far as Vinland to the West, the Caspian Sea to the East and the Mediterranean to the South, there was no need to travel further.

By the end of the 11th century, the days of Viking glory were over. The people of Scandinavia were once more on the fringes of Europe, though Viking blood flowed in millions of Europeans and Asians.

Above *King Harald Bluetooth of Denmark was converted to Christianity after watching a priest called Poppo hold a red-hot bar which did not burn his hands.*

Viking achievements

How should we rate the Vikings and their history? It is not easy to give a firm answer. Other races have excelled them in art and learning, others been notable explorers, others equally skilled in war. Their empire soon became unimportant. Scandinavia was never again to see such an explosion of energy. It was an explosion that at first sight had few permanent results, the Vikings appearing to have been swallowed up by other nations.

Yet in some respects the Vikings have rarely been equalled. It is confidently claimed that they founded Russia and discovered America. They were undoubtedly the greatest explorers and discoverers of their day and, given changing circumstances down the centuries, have never been surpassed. The longship was a masterpiece of craftsmanship. They made beautiful jewellery. They founded states and towns and were some of the keenest and best traders the world has ever known. Among their number ranked not only great warriors, but also great leaders. Canute is a shining example of wise but strong Viking leadership.

One of their greatest qualities was their ability to adapt to new circumstances. In north France, Norse pirate became Norman in hardly more than a generation, and raiders become highly disciplined rulers, soldiers and politicians. Vikings are mostly remembered for terror and cruelty, but it is not a balanced picture. They were in fact a bold and creative people who dominated Europe and the islands of the Atlantic for 300 years.

Opposite *The Vikings were excellent sailors, fierce warriors, skilled craftsmen and keen traders. The illustration shows Thor's hammer; the figure of Canute and his name written in runes; the Vikings as raiders; and Viking women.*

Left *The runes on this memorial stone tell of Danegeld payments made to a Viking who raided England.*

Table of dates

789 First Viking raid on England.

793 Vikings destroy the monastery at Lindisfarne.

860? Naddod discovers Iceland.

863 Vikings from Sweden settle in Novgorod, in what is now Russia.

871 Battle of Ashdown. Vikings defeated by King Ethelred and Alfred.
King Ethelred dies.
Alfred becomes King of Wessex, a large territory in the south-west of England.

878 Battle of Edington. The Viking leader, Guthrum, is defeated by Alfred.
Treaty of Chippenham.
The Danelaw is established.

885 Paris is besieged by Vikings.

890s The Viking 'Great Army' harries the Saxons.

911 A Viking, Rollo, becomes the first Duke of Normandy.

937 Battle of Brunanburh. Vikings and Scots are defeated by King Athelstan.

980s Viking raids are resumed.

982 Erik the Red discovers Greenland.

991 Battle of Maldon. The Saxon Earl Brihtnoth is killed.

994? Canute is born.

1000? Leif Eriksson reaches the New World.

1002 Massacre of St. Brice's Day.

1009 Olaf the Stout destroys London Bridge.

1013 Canute's first visit to England.

1014 Swein Forkbeard, Canute's father, dies.
Battle of Clontarf. Irish defeat the Vikings.

1016 Death of Edmund Ironside.
Canute becomes undisputed King of England.

1018 Canute becomes King of Denmark.

1026 Canute's pilgrimage to Rome.

1030 Battle of Stiklestad. Canute defeats Olaf the Stout and wins control of Norway.

1035 Canute dies.

1066 Battle of Stamford Bridge.
The Viking, Harald Hardrada, is defeated by King Harold of England.

New words

Amber A yellowish-brown fossil used for jewellery.

Archaeology The study of man's past made by digging up and investigating the remnants of his culture.

Burh A Saxon township.

Clinker-built A method of ship-building where the hull is built from planks overlapping the ones below.

Colony A group of people who leave their own land and settle in a distant and unexplored part of the world.

Danegeld Money (geld) paid to the Danes to buy peace. In 1012, Ethelred the Unready handed over 22,000 kg (48,000 lb) of silver to Swein Forkbeard to bribe him to stay away.

Danelaw The area of England under Danish control in the 9th century.

Fjord An inlet of sea carved into the Scandinavian coastline.

Hostage A person who is held captive as a guarantee that promises made by the enemy will be carried out.

Jarl A member of the Viking aristocracy, or a chieftain.

Jester A joker or clown.

Karl A Viking farmer.

Knarr A ship carrying cargo for trading purposes.

Magistrate A person who administers the law in court.

Mariner A sailor.

Mead An alcoholic drink made from honey.

Minstrel A travelling musician or singer.

Monastery A religious house where monks live, work and pray.

Moors People of Arab stock who lived in North Africa and Spain.

Niflheim An imaginary land of snow and mist where Vikings believed they went after their death if they had failed to be brave during their lives.

Orient Countries to the east of the Mediterranean.

Pilgrimage A journey made to a holy place.

Plunder To carry off people's belongings by force.

Portages Carrying boats overland between two rivers.

Relics The holy remains of a saint's body.

Rune A primitive alphabet used by the Vikings.

Saga A story telling the exploits and brave deeds of an hero.

Scandinavia The name given to the territory which included the countries of Denmark, Norway and Sweden.

Skraelings The Viking name given to Eskimos and Red Indians.

Thrall A member of the lowest class of Viking society.

Valhalla The Viking heaven where warriors went after they had died a glorious death in battle.

Valkyries The god Odin's nine daughters who carried the bodies of warriors to Valhalla.

Further information

Places to visit

Museums Every county in Britain has many museums open to the public. It is worth investigating your nearest museum to see if they exhibit any Viking artefacts. Among other treasures, the Museum of London holds a good example of a runic inscription; the British Museum displays a 10th century comb made from bone; the Yorkshire Museum has many Viking artefacts; and you can see the Alfred Jewel in the Ashmolean Museum in Oxford.

Famous sites Naturally there is a wealth of Viking treasures to be seen in Scandinavia. However, it is no longer necessary to travel so far to get an insight into the world of the Vikings. The Jorvik Viking Centre in York is an excellent place to visit. A Viking settlement has been brought to light and painstakingly reconstructed so that you can now take a step back in time and see how the Vikings really lived and worked.

Libraries The local library can always give information about the best places to visit, both near your home and farther afield. Most libraries have a section on local history. Try to discover what was going on in your area during the Viking times.

Books

Crossley-Holland, Kevin, *The Norse Myths* (Penguin 1980)

Ferguson, Sheila, *Growing up in Viking Times* (Batsford)

Gibson, Michael, *The Vikings* (Macdonald)

Gibson, Michael, *The Vikings* (Wayland 1972)

Loyn, Henry, *The Vikings in Britain* (Batsford 1977)

Magnusson, Magnus, *The Vinland Sagas* (Penguin Classics 1965)

Petersen, Palle, *Vikings* (Black)

Purves, Amanda, *Growing up with the Vikings* (Wayland 1978)

Simpson, Jacqueline, *The Viking World* (Batsford 1980)

Wernick, Robert, *The Vikings* (Time-Life Books 1979)

Wood, Michael, *In Search of the Dark Ages* (Ariel Books 1981)

Index

Picture acknowledgements

The illustrations in this book were supplied by: The Jorvik Viking Centre 35, 40; The Mansell Collection 6 (bottom), 19; Topham Picture Library 55. The remaining photographs are from the Wayland Picture Library.